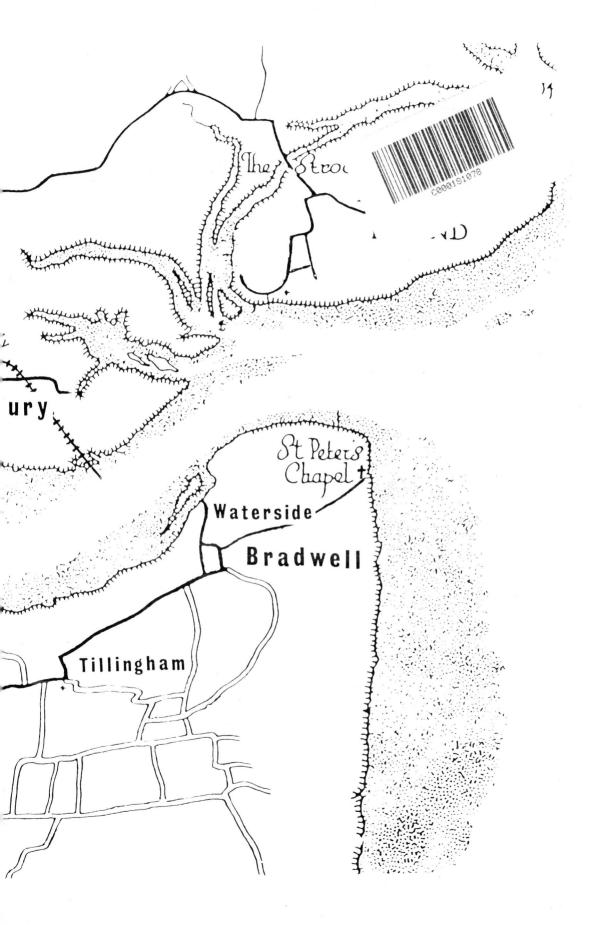

The Stro...

...ND

ury

St Peters
Chapel ✝

Waterside

Bradwell

Tillingham

Maldon
and the
Blackwater Estuary

A Pictorial History

A view of the Moot Hall and the High Street, *c.*1900.

Maldon
and the
Blackwater Estuary
A Pictorial History

John Marriage

Phillimore

1996

Published by
PHILLIMORE & CO. LTD.
Shopwyke Manor Barn, Chichester, West Sussex

First published in 1985
Second edition, 1996

© John Marriage, 1996

ISBN 1 86077 016 9

Printed and bound in Great Britain by
BIDDLES LTD.
Guildford, Surrey

List of Illustrations

Frontispiece: High Street, Maldon at the turn of the century

The seal of the former Borough of Maldon. It has its origins in 1682.

Acknowledgements

These photographs appear by kind permission of the following: T. Atkinson, 111-2, 114; Eric Boesch, 15, 38-9, 44-5, 50, 61, 67, 70-1, 102, 126, 136, 143; Boulton & Paul, 103-4, 106; A.C. Butcher, 116-7, 120-5, 144, 150, 158-60; Eastern National, 145-6; Essex Record Office, 5, 10, 19, 23, 32-5, 46, 53, 56, 63-4, 87, 92-3, 95, 97-8, 100-1, 108, 127, 132, 135, 148, 155, 163, 167; Barbara Ibbotson, 31, 58, 68; E. Lane, 77; Maldon Crystal Salt Co., 109-10; Maldon Museum, 21, 28, 40, 138-9; Maldon Society, 8-9, 12, 16, 20, 25, 151-2; J. Meredith, 72, 141-2; Stanley Sayers, 153, 162; L. Whittaker, 3, 24, 41, 49, 52, 57, 60, 96, 156.

All other photographs and illustrations are supplied from the author's own collection. The endpapers are based on a map by Archie White.

Introduction

Maldon and the Blackwater estuary have always held a special place in my affections. At a very early age I was taken by bus to Mill Beach where I was encouraged to paddle and build sandcastles on the rather muddy foreshore. Later, my wartime schoolboy friends and I would cycle on summer weekends to Maldon for a swim in Marine Lake, which, due to the prevailing travel restrictions, was the nearest one could get to a salt water bathe. No visit was ever complete without a boating trip on the tideway in one of the cumbersome old rowing boats.

Some years later, on taking up canoeing as a hobby, I was able to explore the many fascinating creeks and inlets which fan out from the estuary. Additionally, in my early days as a town planner, my duties included carrying out site surveys at many places near or on the estuary.

Sadly, in pursuing my career, my work subsequently took me away from regular contact with the area. Nevertheless, in 1985, those memories led me to prepare the first edition of this book. Now, over 10 years have elapsed and I find that inevitably substantial changes have taken place. The construction of the Chelmsford A12 bypass has dramatically improved road links with London and south Essex and facilitated the expansion of motor travel within the whole area. Consequently, substantial residential development has taken place at Maldon and the various villages around the estuary. Weekend sailing has increased in popularity and The Hythe, in particular, is now a mecca for sailing barges and other vintage craft. Promenade Park, formerly universally known simply as 'The Rec', has been vastly extended and improved. Local industry has diminished and increasingly shopping facilities within the town are in direct competition with the now well established regional shopping centres at Chelmsford and Colchester. The new Maldon bypass has reduced vehicular congestion on Market Hill and High Street. Nevertheless, both the town and the estuary retain their interest and much of the old world charm survives. The attractive old buildings flanking Market Hill and London Road are particularly to be admired.

This book is a collection of pictures and illustrations of Maldon and the estuary from Victorian times to the 1950s, showing some of the people who lived and worked in those times, and their leisure activities.

Many people helped me in the preparation of this book and I would like in particular to acknowledge the assistance of the Maldon Museum who loaned me many of the pictures and continue to do valuable work in preserving our Essex heritage.

An artist's impression of the Moot Hall and the High Street, *c.*1888.

The Town

MALDON is one of the oldest towns in Essex. Whilst its present history goes back to Saxon times an earlier Romano-British town once existed on flat land to the north side of the river Chelmer, close to what is now Heybridge. When the railway line was excavated in the 19th century Roman remains were spotted. However, little was identified until works were carried out in 1994 prior to intended residential development. These revealed the remains of a substantial town, including evidence of a large temple complex and an extensive market area. Its period of prosperity seems to have straddled the late Iron Age and early Roman period (*c.*50 B.C.-A.D. 200). A major road linked the town to Colchester (Camulodunum) and part still remains in use. However, a presumed route to Chelmsford (Caesaromagus) has yet to be discovered though it is possible that water transport along the Chelmer was used.

It is thought that the settlement was abandoned in the late fifth century, probably the result of rising water levels, which converted the area into marsh and hence into the rough grazing landscape of today.

In A.D. 916 the Saxons established a burh at Maldon on high land to the south of the river Chelmer. They took advantage of its geographical position: a steep hill at the head of a broad estuary and the lowest point at which the two rivers, the Chelmer and the Blackwater, could be crossed. Quickly it became an important town, with a population of about a thousand persons. A royal mint was also established there.

The present London Road bisects the site of the burh. By the Middle Ages the town had expanded to become centred on the original Moot Hall, next to All Saints' Church. At that time it was a market town, serving both the surrounding rural area, and, in addition, trading vessels, which unloaded at a small quay at Fullbridge, where there was a crossing of the river Chelmer. Other cargoes were unloaded downstream at The Hythe, then a separate hamlet, whose wharves were owned by the town. The main road into the town was London Road and this was the normal coach route from Chelmsford and London.

Maldon's great period of economic expansion took place in the 18th century, the result of a general increase in maritime trade. For a time more than half the population was employed in port-related activities, and goods for inland areas were hauled from the town over the steep Danbury Hill.

By 1801, the population had risen to 2,300, whilst at the turn of this century, it was more than five thousand people. To accommodate the increasing population, the area of housing gradually spread from the original high ground southwards towards the little village of Mundon and, leapfrogging over The Causeway, linked with the neighbouring village of Heybridge, itself expanding independently. Former marshes between the two communities became the site of the main industrial and railway complex.

Many medieval buildings in the centre survived this steady expansion, and remain to this day. They included the Moot Hall, the former town hall, which once housed most of the town's civic responsibilities. On the ground floor was the police station, with offices and cells at the rear. On the first floor were the courtrooms for Quarter and Petty Sessions, whilst the Council Chamber was on the second floor.

Nearby in Silver Street is the *Blue Boar Hotel*, which has been a hostelry at least since 1632. Prior to that it was an occasional residence for the Essex family, the De Veres. The inn's sign is derived from the chief heraldic badge of that family. At the front, the building consists of a plain grey brick with a Georgian porchway. At the rear there is a fine 14th-century half-timbered wing and a jumble of other structures. Nearby, in All Saints' churchyard, is buried Lawrence Washington, the great-great-grandfather of George Washington, the first President of the United States of America. Within the church a stained-glass window was unveiled in 1928 in his memory. It was presented by the town of Maldon, Massachusetts, founded in 1649 by emigrants from its Essex namesake.

The earlier workhouse for the district was on Market Hill, and dates back to 1836. It was replaced by the Maldon Union Workhouse in Spital Road in 1873. The original building was subsequently divided into tenements and remains virtually unchanged outside. The newer building is an imposing three-storey, red-brick, slated structure, with a central tower which includes a clock. Its grounds originally ran to five acres and the building housed 350 inmates. A private chapel stands within the grounds adjacent to Spital Road. In 1930 the workhouse became a Public Assistance Institute run by the Essex County Council and in 1948 it became St Peter's Hospital under the National Health Service.

Before the advent of comprehensive education, Maldon had a greatly respected grammar school, founded in 1407, to instruct the sons of fishermen. For a time it was accommodated in Dr. Plume's Library, but was ousted from there in 1817 to make way for the newly established National School, and moved to London Road. In 1907 the school moved to a new building standing in its own grounds in Fambridge Road, where further extensions took place from time to time. When virtually the whole of Essex changed over to comprehensive education, it became the Plume School and more buildings were added.

Prior to modern developments at Chelmsford, Colchester and Basildon as regional centre, Maldon was of greater importance as a shopping and entertainment centres for the whole of the surrounding area and the Dengie peninsula. At the turn of the century Bentall & Sons (a branch of the same family founded the famous store at Kingston-upon-Thames), had an important general outfitter's store at 50, 56 and 58 High Street, with service from the cradle to the grave. Later, Luckin Smith, a Chelmsford-based grocery store, had branches in the locality. The rise of the cooperative movement and strong socialist feelings locally led to the formation of the Maldon and Heybridge Cooperative Society, with various branches in the town and neighbouring villages. This merged with the Colchester Society several years ago. Among the sources of entertainment was a theatre halfway down the High Street and, opening in the 1930s, the Embassy cinema.

The number of public houses has diminished rapidly since the end of the Second World War. Like most market towns and ports, both Maldon and Heybridge had a wealth of such establishments to provide liquid refreshment, sociable company and entertainment. The variety of brews was also much wider than now, with long-forgotten names such as Shrimp Brand, Charrington Nichols, Colchester Brewing Company and, of course, Gray's, a more recent departure as brewers, though they still have houses in the area.

Maldon's most popular area for the holidaymaker is the attractive Recreation Ground and Marine Parade (Promenade Park), developed to its present extent over many years. The first part, with a grand entrance from Mill Road, was opened on 26 June 1895 and, although it started as a bleak and windswept open area, it was developed into a well landscaped park sloping gently down to the water. In 1905 the Marine Lake was formed by blocking off part of the estuary, creating a permanent expanse of salt water next to the original park. Lady Rayleigh performed the opening ceremony. Changing rooms were built, and facilities provided for bathing in the lake. In 1925 Marine Parade was extended over the marshes towards Northey Island, and the Recreation Ground was enlarged in 1926. By the 1950s it had become very popular with visitors, and coachloads of people from East London and various Essex towns would come each weekend. Maldon also became a Mecca for cyclists, who flocked in their dozens to the front. Nowadays, of course, most visitors come by car.

The Estuary

It has been said that there is no area of water in the British Isles like the Blackwater. Certainly, there are no comparable stretches of land-locked salt water to be found elsewhere in the country, unless it be Poole Harbour.

The estuary runs roughly east to west from the North Sea, streaming inland for about seventeen miles, with low lying banks on either side, across which the winds blow freely. For most of its length, until one reaches Northey Island, the deepest channel is along the southern side. At Osea Island the depth of the water is about eighteen feet (three fathoms) in the main channel, but inland it shelves rapidly, and virtually dries out at low tide above Mill Beach. Owing to the wide surface of the estuary and the relatively shallow water, large-scale evaporation takes place through the action of wind and sun, so that the water is saltier than the sea itself.

The mud flats and the surrounding marshes are rich in wildlife, with invertebrates burrowing in the mud providing a source of food for fish and wading birds. The Blackwater and the other Essex estuaries are of international importance as an overwintering area for waders and wildfowl—both ducks and geese. Five per cent of the world's population of these fowl can be found in the estuary at certain times.

In the past fishing was of considerable importance, and inshore boats caught in particular herrings and sprats, as well as plaice, sole and cod. The oyster fisheries in this area have a high reputation for producing quality shellfish.

Throughout history, the Blackwater has been extensively navigated. At a time when few roads or tracks existed, early Celtic inhabitants of the region used it as a highway. At a later date, the Roman town at Heybridge developed into a substantial trading post which had links with the continent. Roman vessels would have passed to and from Heybridge, protected by the garrison at Othono. The Saxons entered Essex via the estuary both as foragers and later as settlers. Later, the Vikings made their marauding trips up the estuary and one of their most famous battles against the Saxons took place on the waterside. Tradition says that they beached their longboats on Northey Island, and fighting took place on a narrow causeway linking it to the mainland, where the Saxons were assembled. As only a few warriors could be engaged at a time, the fighting was inconclusive and so, foolhardily, the Saxons agreed to withdraw to the higher ground behind the estuary where they were defeated by superior fighters. Among those killed was Byrhtnoth, the Saxon Earl of Essex. His statue is in the wall of All Saints' Church at Maldon.

Subsequently, in medieval times, the river was used extensively by a variety of craft for trade. Later, however, larger colliers and schooners were unable to penetrate as far as either Maldon or Heybridge, because of shallow water, and their cargoes were off-loaded into lighters near Northey Island. Sailing barges, though, unique to the east coast, were able to nose their way up the narrow side creeks to serve nearby villages and isolated farms. Nevertheless, despite this limited draught, many cargoes arrived at Maldon, to be delivered into the Essex hinterland by heavy and cumbersome waggons and pack mules.

The estuary was used increasingly for recreation during the Victorian era. The wealthy had steam and sailing yachts based on the river, whilst railway transport enabled working-class people from London and other Essex towns to visit the area for a day or so. More visitors arrived as bus and coach services to Maldon and other places along the estuary expanded. It was during this period that Mill Beach, Steeple and Maylandsea became popular weekend resorts, with large numbers of caravans and weekend homes, whilst the visitors enjoyed themselves in or on the water.

The two estuary islands were once of similar size. Osea Island extended to about 330 acres, whilst Northey Island was slightly larger with 335 acres. Most of Northey Island is low lying and, as the sea walls are broken, most has reverted to salt marshes and is now mainly the haunt of wildfowl. The only house on the island is partially on stilts, which gave its former owner, Sir Norman Angell, Nobel prize winner in 1933, a view of practically the whole island.

Higher and farther down the estuary, Osea Island is now a farm, but it has had a varied history. It was once owned by Mr. Frederick Charrington of the brewing family. He developed it as a temperance resort, mainly for middle-class people from London. In 1914 it was taken over by the Royal Navy and during the Great War was an important naval base, where over two thousand sailors were stationed. Most were billeted in temporary huts which were removed after the war. Some huts were re-erected at Mill Beach and converted into homes, and several are still there.

In 1913 a little-known piece of aviation history took place at Osea when the British Deperdussin Aeroplane Company tested a newly-developed seaplane. The aeroplane was a single-engine monoplane, fitted with two large floats, and it took off on the south side of the island in the deep water channel. It was piloted by the managing director of the company, Lieut. Porte, R.N., who took the plane on a successful 10-minute flight.

In the Second World War the island was occupied by the army.

During the several periods this century of world-wide recession the head of the estuary has been a popular place for mooring tankers and general cargo vessels until they could be recommissioned. Thus, rusting hulks, swinging gently on their anchors, have become a familiar sight, whilst skeleton crews carry out only basic maintenance. This is perhaps the least positive of man's activities on the estuary.

Villages around the Blackwater

A number of villages surround the Blackwater estuary. On the north bank are Tollesbury, Tolleshunt D'Arcy and Goldhanger and on to the south are Bradwell, Tillingham, Steeple and Mundon. Each to a lesser or greater degree has links with the estuary.

Tollesbury is located on a creek leading off the lower end of the estuary and is a picturesque place, built around a central square. Nikolaus Pevsner in his book *The Buildings of England: Essex* describes it as being a little town rather than a village. Situated on the edge of the saltings, its links with the sea go back a thousand years. Once it was mainly a fishing community, specialising in oysters. In the last century over fifty smacks were employed in the locality, dredging and laying. All had crews from the village. Nevertheless, it was also a port for the area and at one time coal came by sea to the hard to be loaded into carts and sold at 16s. 0d. a ton to the locals. More recently, yachting has become an important activity, and the front is usually crowded with boats in a very pleasant setting of mellow timber sails lofts at the water edge.

Tillingham is purely an agricultural village some way from the water, while Bradwell really consists of two separate villages. Bradwell juxta Mare is about a mile from the estuary and, like Tillingham, mainly agricultural in origin. Bradwell Lodge, right in the village facing Bradwell church, is a noted building. It was built in the early 16th century and was originally a moated manor house with a Georgian wing added in 1785. Until 1938 it was the rectory, when it was sold to Tom Driberg, the journalist and later the Member of Parliament for the former Maldon constituency. He made it his home until 1970, although during the war it served as the Officers' Mess for the nearby wartime airfield (on the site now occupied by a power station), with Nissen hunts on the lawn for extra accommodation. Bradwell Waterside, next to Bradwell Creek, is a small community which has grown up around the quay which once served the surrounding agricultural area. Here 'stackies' would be loaded, to be sailed to London along with other farm products. Although now almost totally given over to yachting, it was once the home port of the Parker fleet of 26 Thames barges, including *Lord Warden* and *Nellie Parker*. The sailing families of the Spittys and Kirbys lived in cottages nearby.

Now a place of pilgrimage, St Peter's-on-the-Wall, a small barn-like structure at the mouth of the estuary, in a bleak, windswept spot overlooking the North Sea, has a long history. During the first century, the Romans built a large fort called Othono there, as a defence against marauding Saxons. When the Roman legions were withdrawn, the fort became derelict, but in 654 St Cedd established a mission in Essex, and built a church astride the landward side of the old fort, making much use of original Roman material. In time, its Christian use lapsed, and the small structure became firstly a beacon and later a barn, and part of the nave wall was destroyed to allow farm carts to enter. In 1920 the building was taken over by a group of trustees, as a gift to the Diocese of Chelmsford. The old roof was made watertight, the floor paved, the walls repaired, and the whole restored to a place of Christian heritage.

Industry

As in most long-established English towns, there is a long industrial tradition in Maldon. Old established enterprises included boat and barge building, salt manufacturing, brewing and flour milling. The motive power for the latter was water or wind, but later, steam roller milling, fuelled by coal, was invented, so that larger capacity mills could be built beside the estuary, using water solely for transportation. Other industries established during the industrial revolution also settled in the town, including the Maldon Ironworks, whose factory was built in 1875 after moving from Heybridge, Sadd's Timber Works and other firms.

A most remarkable industry, which completely dominated Heybridge for 150 years, was E.H. Bentall & Co. Ltd., founded in 1795 by William Bentall, a Goldhanger yeoman farmer. As a sideline to farming he built a foundry, smith and joinery shop next to his farm. From there he designed, built and sold to local farmers a plough, most advanced for its day. Sales were so successful that he decided to quit farming and concentrate on their manufacture. For this purpose he moved to Heybridge in 1805, next to the newly-dug Chelmer and Blackwater Canal, to transport his raw materials. The 'Goldhanger' plough—as it continued to be called—was the mainstay of his business, though other agricultural equipment was made.

His son, Edward Hammond Bentall, a great innovator, took over the business in 1836, and under him it continued to expand with sales all over Britain and its developing colonies. Concurrently with the expansion of trade, Bentall constructed nearby his own house, called The Towers. Its walls were made entirely of concrete blocks and it is believed to have been the first building to use reinforced concrete in its construction. About the same time he erected several rows of workers' cottages using similar materials. Whilst providing sound, if small, accommodation, they were incredibly ugly and in later years suffered from dampness. The Towers was dynamited in the 1950s to make way for a housing estate.

In 1889 the firm was taken over by his son, Edmund Ernest Bentall, who continued his father's policy of expansion, and at the turn of the century started to make motor cars. They were not a financial success for the firm, although for the time and the price no better cars were then being built in Britain. About a hundred were made before production was discontinued. Nevertheless, the experience gained in engine design was not wasted, as the firm went on to sell thousands of small petrol and paraffin engines.

At its peak, in 1914, the firm employed nearly 7,000 people and during the Great War produced shell cases, in addition to routine work. In the Second World War parts were made for the Handley Page 'Halifax' bombers, including tail fins and bomb doors, as well as agricultural machinery. Employment over this period was 1,000 men and women.

John Sadd Ltd. (now taken over by Boulton & Paul of Norwich) was a very long-established firm. Apparently, the first John Sadd was a Chelmsford carpenter who moved to Maldon in 1729 and set up business there. Successive generations, each of whose eldest son was named John, followed, in turn developing the business. The firm, near Fullbridge, specialised mainly in providing timber and material for the building trade, but for a time they were also shipowners and wharfingers. Timber was imported direct from the continent. As one of their secondary activities, from 1912 to 1931 they supplied the entire electricity supply for Maldon and Heybridge until this was taken over by the local electricity supply company. During the Great War the company made wooden huts and accessories for the War Department, which led to post-war expansion of the joinery side of the business. During the Second World War the company again built army huts, together with a wide variety of small boats, assault craft and pontoons, as well as aircraft parts.

The town is still the host for one of the oldest industries in the world—that of salt making. At Maldon, salt is still made by the traditional method of collecting sea water in huge pans and allowing the water to evaporate, leaving behind pure salt crystals. It is interesting to note that in 1086 Domesday Book records that 45 salt pans existed in the Maldon area alone. Today, only the small factory in Downs Road survives. Its products are sold in health food and delicatessen shops throughout Britain and many parts of the world.

Another unusual industry was operated by May and Butcher at Heybridge Basin. They combined a shipping business with the manufacture of sheds and agricultural equipment. Ships of many kinds were broken up by them, including HMS *Dido*, a 5,600-ton light cruiser. This vessel had been launched in 1896 and was one of the nine ships in the 'Eclipse' class, all of which had a top speed of 19 knots. After service in the Great War, *Dido* was brought up the Blackwater and scrapped by May and Butcher in 1926. Although ship-breaking ended just prior to the Second World War, the manufacturing side of the business continued until 1984.

Fishing has played an important part in Maldon's long history. Most of the vessels were designed with a shallow stern, of use when hauling in dredging nets for oyster and other shellfish. When not in use these vessels have always been moored in a line along the waterside at The Hythe. This industry has been in the hands of several local families for generations. Best known are the Hedgecocks, Pitts and Wrights.

As may be expected from the town's historic connection with the sea, a condition of the first charter was that a ship should be provided for the King's Defence, and consequently from time to time boats have been supplied to the Royal Navy. Even as recently as 1940, little ships sailed from the estuary to help in the evacuation of Dunkirk. It is not surprising, therefore, that boat building has carried on at The Hythe for a very long time. Cook's boatyard was established there in the latter part of the 19th century, and is now well-known as a builder of numerous small craft. In the past it also built other vessels, including the well-known Thames barge *Dawn*. The firm specialises in the repair of Thames barges, which are moored, whilst under repair, in the mud berths nearby.

Transport

Although the heyday of both rail and canal have come and gone, both have left a heavy imprint on the geography of Maldon and Heybridge, whilst farther down the estuary, at Tollesbury, there are also limited remians of an old railway.

Construction of the Chelmer and Blackwater Navigation followed an enabling Act of Parliament in 1793. Basically, it involved making the river Chelmer navigable from Chelmsford to Maldon. Its object was to allow Chelmsford to enjoy the advantages of water transport and not rely on heavy waggons using the muddy roads of the time. In this it was successful, and encouraged industry and commerce to become established in the county town. At Maldon, owing to short-sighted opposition from the Town Council, the canal had to be constructed entirely outside the old Borough boundary. For this reason an artificial channel was made from Beeleigh down to what is now Heybridge Basin, discharging into the estuary opposite Northey Island. There a small port was constructed as an alternative to the original planned terminus of the navigation at Fullbridge. The sea lock at Heybridge Basin was built large enough to take vessels up to 300 tons, whilst the remainder of the navigation was able to take lighters 60-feet long with a cargo of 30 tons. The waterway was very active and Heybridge Basin busy with colliers and schooners until the construction of the railways, when traffic gradually declined. During this period Bentall's and other firms at Heybridge used the canal to import raw materials by water. After the construction of the railway, the Basin was used more as a laying-up place for yachts and other pleasure craft, which still continues. The remainder of the canal is now used for recreation of all kinds; motor cruising, canoeing, angling, and rambling along the old towpath.

Although after the construction of the canal Maldon ceased to be a port for Chelmsford, it continued to serve Witham and Braintree. In 1845 the first steps were taken to promote a railway from Braintree to Maldon. Two years later work on the new railway started and on Monday 2 October 1848, it was opened. The original idea had been to build a direct line from Braintree, through Witham, to Maldon. Instead, it was built in the form of two branches, each leaving the main line at Witham for Braintree and Maldon respectively. In future years this discouraged through trains. The Maldon line was laid as a double track, but one was removed and sold to the War Department for use in the Crimea.

The passenger station at Maldon was a most elaborate building for the size of the town. It was built in the Queen Anne style with large adjoining goods yards. The railway never fully developed its intended rôle of carrying goods direct from the boats to Braintree, as a large dock planned next to the station was never completed. Instead, a modest connecting spur and quay was made at its crossing with the canal, so that goods coming by water for Braintree could be floated up from Heybridge Basin and transferred to the railway waggons at the little quay. Later, Bentall's made use of the same wharf when coal started to come by rail instead of coasters.

In October 1889 another line was constructed to Maldon. This left the Liverpool Street-Southend line at Wickford. Another passenger station and goods yard were built at Maldon West, and a connection made by way of a viaduct and bridge over the river Chelmer to the older station, which was renamed Maldon East. At the turn of the century trains took 85 minutes to reach Liverpool Street via Witham and 82 minutes via Shenfield. Altogether there were 13 trains to London each weekday, including a reduced service on Sundays. A large amount of freight was also carried, including market garden produce. It is recorded that on 11 July 1891, using both stations, 925 tons of green peas were sent to London in 313 trucks.

Both lines were used extensively in both the First and Second World Wars, although passengers were withdrawn from the Maldon West line in September 1939. All traffic ceased on this line on 1 April 1953, followed by the closure of the Witham line on 7 September 1964.

For a time, a further line served the Blackwater estuary. This was the Kelvedon, Tiptree and Tollesbury Railway. It was built by the Great Eastern Railway Company in 1904 and extended to Tollesbury Pier in 1907. The intention was to tap the developing interest in the Blackwater as a holiday and boating resort. For a time, the famous steam launch *Maldon Annie* landed passengers at the pier. Although busy for a time, trade never came up to expectations, and the services were cut back to Tollesbury Town station in 1921. The line to the pier was temporarily re-opened during the Second World War to carry supplies to gun emplacements along the sea wall. The pier itself, however, had a hole blown in it to prevent any possible use by the Germans, and was finally demolished after the war. Passenger services to Tollesbury were withdrawn in 1950 and the whole line closed from October 1962. Passenger trains on this line consisted of quaint little carriages, with open verandahs at either end, from which travellers could view the countryside as the train puffed slowly along.

The Maldon East station building still survives and is now the most substantial reminder of the railways which once served Maldon and the Blackwater. The route of the former track between Maldon West and East stations has been replaced by the Maldon bypass which has obliterated all signs of the extensive railway cuttings and embankments. However, as on other lines, blue engineering bricks were used as facing materials to the bridges and this tradition has been deliberately repeated on the new bypass bridges as an echo and tribute to the old railway.

The period between the wars saw the development of coach and bus services throughout the area. The main operators were the Chelmsford-based Eastern National Bus Company, which built a bus station in Maldon High Street to a similar style as others they built elsewhere in Essex. Other services were operated by private companies—Moores of Kelvedon, who started business as general carriers, and Osbornes of Tollesbury. Today, although there are still services by both Eastern National and Osbornes, the main means of transport is the motor car.

For many people the bicycle was the only form of transport available, and the comparatively flat terrain was ideal for its use. Many visitors to Maldon and the estuary, particularly between the wars, would come on their bicycles, bound for the rather muddy beaches. Many came as members of the Cyclist Touring Club or local clubs. Local people also found cycles ideal for getting to work or generally getting about, and there were few people who did not own a 'bike'. Special cycle shops were sited in strategic locations in Maldon High Street and various villages. Many provided a real service, staying open at all hours for emergency repairs, including mending punctures, and also providing a place for visitors to park them temporarily during a visit to the area.

Maldon

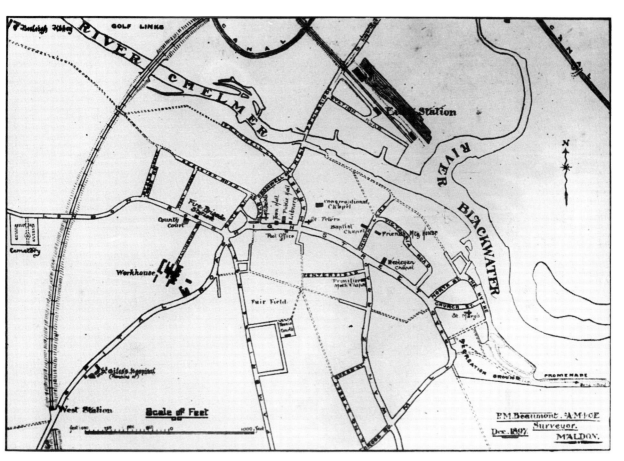

1 Plan of the town of Maldon, 1897.

2 The Fullbridge and Market Hill as they appeared in 1830. A sea-going vessel is being unloaded at the town quay and a well laden cart stands nearby. *The Angel* public house later became *The Welcome Sailor*.

3 High Street, in 1850: a very elegant thoroughfare. A horse-drawn omnibus has turned into Market Hill, perhaps heading towards the newly opened railway station.

4 The Maldon publishers, Gowers Ltd., capture for ever a busy summer early this century, with pedestrians, cyclists and horse-drawn traffic going about their business.

5 The Moot Hall, photographed about 1900, has changed little externally. Once it housed the police station, and the shadowy figure of a bobby can just be spied under the portico. A new police station was subsequently built elsewhere.

Moot Hall, Maldon.

6 This 1900 view from the Moot Hall roof reveals the interesting medieval rooftops of buildings lining the High Street.

7 High Street at four o'clock on a summer afternoon, with varied forms of transport in use. A bath chair, bicycle, pony and trap, waggon and donkey cart can all be seen.

8 Looking towards West Square, with Wentworth House in the centre of the picture. The beautiful tree disappeared soon after the Great War when the police station was built in the garden, facing the square.

9 High Street during the Great War. Soldiers lounge near the Moot Hall, while a mounted officer, with a remount, passes by.

10 (*above*) Looking down the High Street, *c*.1920. The first building on the left, now known as Church House, constructed about 1700, became the home of Edward Bright later that century. In his youth, he was a post boy, and rode daily to and from Chelmsford. He is reputed to have been the largest man ever to have lived in England, weighing nearly 42 stones. He is buried in All Saints' churchyard.

11 (*above*) Inter-war High Street.

12 (*left*) Marshland sheep turn down Market Hill, with the aid of a drover and his border collie, probably on their way to Maldon East railway station and hence to the London markets.

13 & 14 These two pictures of the High Street, with St Peter's tower in the background, are separated by 40 years. At the turn of the century only one gas lamp was visible to illuminate the street and the horse-drawn carts and vehicles are typical of the era. The motor car dominates the second picture. Notice more modern shop fronts, electric lighting and just a glimpse of a motor bike.

15 An almost timeless view of Silver Street and the *Blue Boar Hotel*. Only the car dates the picture to *c.*1950.

16 Well-lopped trees shade the entrance to the Methodist church in lower High Street. The shadows under the shop blinds set the time at high noon.

17 Copy of an advertisement which appeared about 1890.

BLUE BOAR HOTEL,

Commercial & Posting House,

MALDON, ESSEX.

E. S. Hickford, Proprietress,

Coffee and Private Rooms. Excellent
House for Cyclists, Tourists, &c.

MODERATE   CHARGES.

HOT JOINTS 1.30 DAILY.

CHOICE WINES AND SPIRITS.

Well Appointed Billiard Room.

CARRIAGES OF EVERY DESCRIPTION FOR HIRE.

Omnibus attends Trains.

Glass Funeral Car, Hearse and Mourning Coaches.

COOD STABLING.   LOOSE BOXES.

18 Customers outside the *White Horse Hotel* at the turn of the
century.

19 One of the first cars in the town leaves the *Swan Hotel*.

20 Telegraph boys in smart uniforms and caps outside the post office, which in those days was opposite the later building in the High Street.

21 Black Norfolk turkeys, now virtually extinct, adorn Bunting's butcher's shop in the High Street about 1910. Carcasses of the less unusual pork and lamb are also on display.

22 Copy of an 1890 advertisement for Orttewell and Son Ltd. Their shop was just a few doors away from the Moot Hall.

23 Market Hill, *c*.1900, leading down to
Fullbridge, the only river crossing in the town.
The steep, gravelled road caused problems
for horse-drawn traffic and, for the benefit of
very heavy waggons travelling up the hill,
extra horses were available for hire from
stables at the bottom. Most of the buildings
in the picture still survive. The large building
on the left was the local workhouse until 1875.

24 Fullbridge at about the same date. The bridge, built about 1825, is marked by the slight hump in the road surface. After a long period of disuse, when traffic was diverted via a temporary bridge built alongside, it was demolished in 1960 and replaced by the present structure.

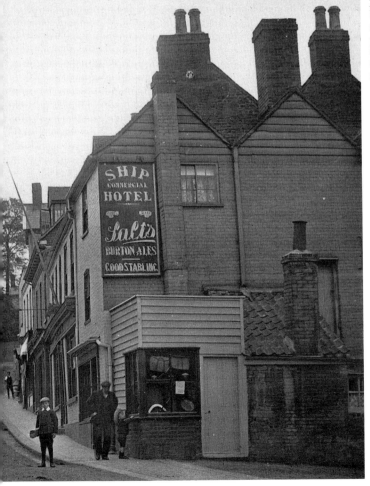

25 Market Hill seen from the bridge early this century. This view is virtually unchanged and one of the most attractive in the town, although the steep incline is still a problem for traffic.

26   Spital Road, *c*.1900, its quiet rural character as yet unaffected by change.

27   The photographer has been able to persuade passers-by in Spital Road to pose for the camera, adding interest to a picture of an otherwise very quiet thoroughfare.

28 Lovers Walk, Beeleigh, *c.*1910. 'And little pathways sweet to see go seeking sweeter places yet.' (John Clare, 1793-1864.)

29 A sketch showing the interior of St Giles Leper Hospital in Spital Road, when it was used as a barn. The roof collapsed about 1910, and the ruins are now preserved.

Lion Tree, Beeleigh.

30 This unusual deformity on the side of an elm tree, formerly growing in a hedgerow near Beeleigh Mill, was much admired by Victorians, who dubbed it the Lion Tree.

31 Beeleigh Abbey, pictured here about 1905, was founded by Premonstratensian monks in 1180 and continued until 1540. Since the Reformation it has been used as a family house.

32 At the turn of the century these properties in Wantz Road were elegant private houses. Much altered and renovated, they now comprise a single guest house.

33 Two Victorian ladies taking the air on a summer's day in the garden of a house adjoining St Mary's Church.

34 & 35 The Maldon Grammar School occupied a two-storey building in London Road from 1817 until 1907, when it moved to new premises in Fambridge Road. Now the original school is in residential use while its successor is the Plume School, and has been considerably enlarged.

36 This advertisement appeared in 1895. At that time townspeople sent their sons here for a good all-round education.

37 Photographed from the top of St Mary's Church, this popular event is believed to be the opening of the Marine Lake.

38 *The Jolly Sailor* at The Hythe—well sited for thirsty mariners.

39 Two young visitors enjoying a 'half o' brown' soon after the Second World War. A similar drink awaits the photographer.

40 A chauffeur-driven motor car approaches the entrance to the Recreation Ground, now Promenade Park, soon after its opening in 1895. At that time the newly planted trees gave very sparse protection from summer sun and the chilly winter east winds.

41 The imposing entrance a few years later. The notice on the right-hand pillar bears witness to the problem of the motor car.

42 A school party walks briskly along the path skirting Marine Lake, in those days lacking the trees which now offer shelter from the keen winds.

43 Maldon in its heyday. A typical scene in high summer when, between the wars, hundreds of holidaymakers would crowd into the Recreation Ground to relax by the edge of Marine Lake.

44 A panoramic view of Marine Lake about the same year, showing the toddlers' paddling area. Many of the buildings edging the crescent were built at the same time as the lake and most still remain.

45 A summer day about 1950. Probably an east breeze was keeping bathers from the water! Much better to enjoy a 'cuppa'!

46 Here, at the turn of the century, the wooden swimming platform and diving board at the deep end of Marine Lake is a source of interest to spectators at the water's edge.

47 (*top left*) The former railway viaduct and bridge over the river Chelmer, upstream of Maldon, seen here about 1950. The centre span was removed for safety reasons in the 1960s and the remainder of the structure demolished and replaced by the present Maldon bypass in the 1980s.

48 (*above*) 'Messing about in boats'. Children then, as now, enjoy nothing more. The Hythe is seen from the enclosing wall of Marine Lake.

49 (*left*) The motor boat *Conqueror* waits at anchor for a full complement of passengers. In 1940 she served the nation, rescuing soldiers from the beaches at Dunkirk.

50 The shallow water is emphasised as the yachtsman wades across the channel at low tide.

51 The Promenade in the 1920s was, as now, a popular place to stroll along the waterside and take the air. Surprisingly in those days beach tents were apparently available to encourage estuary swimmers, who must have been prepared to brave the strong current and foreshore mud rather than enjoy the relative comfort of the nearby swimming pool.

Heybridge and Mill Beach

52 A young lady makes her way towards the busy little shopping centre at The Square, *c.*1920. The owner of the sports car is probably inside the *Half Moon* with a glass of the now vanished brand of Shrimp beers and ales.

53 The older development in Heybridge Street contrasts starkly with the terraced workers' cottages in Hall Road, which had something of the appearance of a northern wool town.

54 Heybridge Street, still with the air of a village, busy with horse-drawn vehicles. In those days, the road was merely gravelled and in dry weather it was necessary to settle the dust by water sprinkling.

55 Heybridge church, *c*.1890.

56 Another view of Heybridge Street about 1900, from the junction of Hall Road, with Bentall's factory in the distance.

57 Prosperous suburban houses on Holloway Road, built about 1900. The beautiful wrought-iron railings were removed in the early 1940s and melted down to assist the war effort.

58 Heybridge Hall Farm, wedged between the canal and Heybridge Creek, seen about 1905. In recent years the farm and surrounding land have become a holiday camp, and the rural tranquillity captured here has long gone.

59 Built in 1873 in an Italianate style, The Towers at Heybridge was the home of Mr. E.H. Bentall and was set in a beautiful landscaped garden. Together with the surrounding boundary wall and lodge, it was constructed in reinforced concrete, Bentall being a pioneer in the use of this material. The house was destroyed in the early 1960s and, together with its gardens, replaced by the present housing estate.

60 A general view of Heybridge Basin from the sea wall, *c*.1905. A ramshackle cottage stands on the isolated spit of land, which has now been entirely built on.

61 The Chelmer and Blackwater Navigation has always supported a resident population of mute swans, a protected bird. Here adult birds are protecting their newly hatched cygnets.

62 A sketch, drawn in 1880, depicting the *Mill Beach Hotel* and the windmill which, together with the nearby tide mill, gave its name to the locality. Already derelict, the windmill had lost two sails and was demolished soon afterwards.

63 Even before the Great War Mill Beach was a popular spot for holidaymakers. Apart from the hotel and a few bathing huts, no other facilities existed.

The Estuary

The Blackwater, Maldon

64 Prior to 1905, looking down the estuary from St Mary's Church tower, with Northey Island in the distance. Although Marine Parade already exists, Marine Lake is still part of the estuary.

65 The Thames sailing barge *Dawn*, seen here at Maldon in 1934, has had a chequered career. She was built in 1897 by Walter Cook and Arthur Woodard at Bath Wall Yard, Maldon, for James Keeble of Cross Road, and used as a stackie. After the Great War she was sold to Francis and Gilders Ltd. of Colchester for general cargo work. Later she went to Brown & Son Ltd. of Chelmsford, who dismasted her for use as a dumb lighter carrying timber between Osea Island and Heybridge Basin. In 1966 she was acquired by Gordon Swift who refitted and converted her into a charter vessel. Subsequently she was acquired by the Passmore Edwards Museum of Stratford for use by parties of under-privileged children, but is now undergoing an extensive refit.

66 *Dawn* flying Gordon Swift's personal pennant.

67 The side creeks and inlets off the Blackwater are littered with the wreckage of old vessels, many of which have been there for a considerable time. These remains just off Mill Beach are thought to have been there for over thirty years at the time this picture was taken.

68 In operation before the Great War making regular trips from Maldon to the mouth of the estuary, steamboat *Annie* is even now remembered with affection. Here she is seen leaving the town, full of passengers.

THE FAVOURITE SEA TRIPS

OF THE

S.S. "ANNIE,"

To Osea Island, West Mersea & Bradwell-on-Sea, from the Hythe Quay.

FARES: Maldon to Osea, single 6d., return 9d;
Sea Trips 4d. extra; Maldon to West Mersea or
Bradwell-on-Sea, Return 2.-; Osea to West Mersea
or Bradwell, return 1/-

				Leave Osea
Aug. 9	F	9.30 a.m.	Day trip to Osea and Bradwell-on-Sea, leave Osea 11, leave Bradwell 4.30.	7.30 ,,
,, 10	S	10.0 a.m.	Day trip to Osea and West Mersea. Leave Osea 11.0, leave Mersea 5.30	8.0 ,,
,, 12	M	10.0 a.m.	Trip to Osea, with Sea trip or 2 hours ashore.	1.0 ,,
,, 13	Tu	11.0 a.m.	Trip to Osea with Trip round Island or 2 hours ashore ...	2.0 ,,
,, 14	W	11.45 a.m. First trip. 2.0 p.m. Second trip.		
,, 15	Th	12.30 p.m.	Trip to Osea with trip round Island or 2 hrs. ashore	3.30 ,,
,, 16	F	1.15 p.m. First trip. 3.15 p.m. Second trip.		
,, 17	S	2.0 p.m. First trip. 4.0 p.m. Second trip.		
,, 19	M	3.30 p.m.	Trip to Osea with Sea trip or 1½ hours ashore.	5.45 ,,
,, 20	Tu	4.15 p.m.	Trip to Osea with Sea trip or 1½ hrs. ashore.	6.45 ,,
,, 21	W	5.0 p.m. First trip. p.m. Second trip.		

Further particulars may be obtained of the Owner's
Agents:—
SPURGEON & SON, MALDON.

69 August 1912: sailing schedule of the steamboat *Annie*.

70 Foreign timber being off-loaded from a German coaster into dumb lighters about 1950. When the operation was complete the string was towed upstream either to John Sadd's wharf at Maldon or Brown & Son's warehouse at Heybridge Basin.

71 In the 1950s canoeing was increasing as a popular sport, and young paddlers used home-built craft made from lathes and canvas. These frail boats often ventured down the estuary. Here a group has landed on mud flats to view laid-up cargo vessels.

72 Tollesbury Pier, a gaunt structure, provided access for railway passengers to river craft. It was partly demolished during the Second World War.

73 This picture of the hardway to Osea Island was taken about 1905, and it has changed little over the years. Completely submerged at every tide, it is not a route to be attempted when the tide is coming in, and it remains a trap for the unwary.

Rivermere, Osea Island.

74 & 75 Early this century Osea Island was run as a temperance resort, and visitors stayed in a large house known as Rivermere.

76 Also on Osea Island there was a tiny village with a general store.

77 The farmhouse on Northey Island, prior to its purchase by Sir Norman Angell. He extended the buildings and planted the first trees on the island.

Villages — north side

78 Fish Street, Goldhanger, leads to the estuary and, formerly, to a decoy pond for waterfowl. This photograph, taken in 1912, shows the typical gravelled roads of the area.

79 A horseless carriage approaches the road junction at Tolleshunt D'Arcy. The popularity of wildfowling is evidenced by the sign 'Cartridges' displayed in the window of the shop, which is also apparently an agent for bicycles.

80 & 81 (*right and below*) Tollesbury, a village located next to the estuary and surrounded by farmland and saltings, has always been surprisingly urban in character. Even the names of the principal streets reflect this—High Street, West Street, East Street and Church Street. Here are two views of the village at the turn of the century, when adults and children could converse and walk in the middle of the road in perfect safety.

Church Street, Tollesbury.

82 (*below*) This unusual photograph, across the flat green countryside towards the marshes and the estuary, was taken in 1920 from the top of Tollesbury church. The long row of houses stretching into the distance marks the line of the road to the waterside and Mell House.

83 Graces, at Tollesbury, is everyone's idea of a perfect country cottage.

84 Guisnes Court, Tollesbury, a splendid 30-room private house, seen here about 1900. By the end of the Great War it had become dilapidated but was restored in the 1930s by William Hurlestone-Horton, who purchased the house and the surrounding estate. More recently, after a spell as an old people's home and a hotel, it became a country club.

85 Coastguard cottages at Tollesbury earlier this century.

86 Fishing boats and their tenders wait for the tide at Woodrope Hard, Tollesbury. Although the creek leads off the Blackwater estuary the boats are registered at Colne, hence the prefix CK.

87 Waiting for the tide at Tollesbury; fishermen make busy preparations.

Villages — south side

88   At Tillingham, as at Steeple, there was little to fear from passing traffic, and the village children were able to pose in complete safety for the photographer.

89   Between the wars the increasing number of motor cars enabled Londoners to make weekend visits to the estuary and enjoy boating from previously inaccessible places like Maylandsea.

90 At the turn of the century, unlike today, holiday traffic was not a problem in the village street at Steeple.

91 Pictured here about 1905, this row of weather-boarded properties faces the estuary across the large green. A decorative verandah offers some protection from the north-east winds.

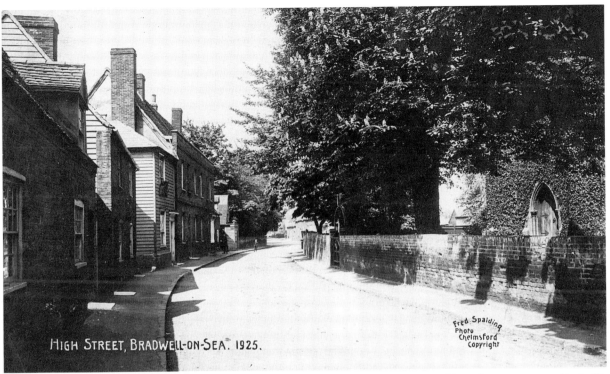

HIGH STREET, BRADWELL-ON-SEA. 1925.

Fred Spalding
Photo
Chelmsford
Copyright

92 The attractive High Street at Bradwell, *c.*1910, with St Thomas' Church on one side and cottages opposite, built from locally-made red bricks or weather board over a timber frame, often painted white.

93 Another view of Bradwell High Street, showing the post office attractively framed by a large chestnut tree. A solitary motor car stands outside a small shop.

94 The sturdy War Memorial at Bradwell stands tribute to the fallen from this village in the Great War.

95 The elegant country house, Down Hall, seen here about 1910.

DOWN HALL, BRADWELL-ON-SEA. 1920.

96 A Thames barge at Bradwell waterside unloads at the little quay, *c.*1910. An empty vessel is moored nearby.

97 The *May Flower* takes on cargo of corn and other farm produce at Bradwell waterside.

98 The coastguard station at Bradwell seen from the quay, *c.*1914. The photographer was clearly the subject of some curiosity as the two locals and a well-dressed lady watched his every move.

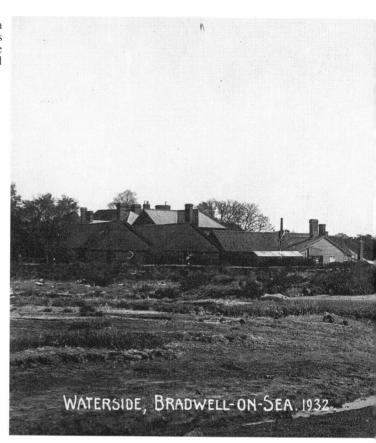

WATERSIDE, BRADWELL-ON-SEA. 1932.

99 The village street at Bradwell waterside, 1910. A horse-drawn delivery van stands outside *The Green Man*.

WATERSIDE, BRADWELL-ON-SEA. 1935.

Fred Spalding
Photo
Chelmsford
Copyright

100 The quaint little shop and post office at the top of the village street at about the same date as the previous picture.

101   Prior to the Great War, the ancient chapel of St Peter's-on-the-Wall lapsed into use as a farm barn. In this picture well-dressed visitors pick their way gingerly through the farmyard to inspect the interior.

Industry

102 Live eels were imported via Heybridge Basin for sale on the London streets. They were shipped in floating containers from Northern Europe and crated up at the quayside.

103 This fascinating aerial photograph, taken in the second quarter of this century, shows the former Potman marsh, now Maldon's main industrial and commercial area. The Causeway runs from left to right in the picture, and in the foreground are the extensive works of John Sadd's. Behind Sadd's complex is the busy Maldon East railway station, and the derelict uncompleted dock immediately to the right, with the track stretching into the distance towards Witham. Heybridge Mill can be seen in the top right-hand corner, and the former Maldon Iron Works on the left-hand side of the picture.

104 Sadd's Wharf in 1900. Workmen unloading sawn timber from sailing barges into quayside warehouses.

105 John Sadd's sawmills, 1900.

106 Men and women busy at work assembling craft for the Armed Forces at Sadd's during the Second World War.

107 The brigantine *Wave* was built at Maldon during the first part of the 19th century. Her owner, John Sadd, employed her in the lucrative coastal trade, and a weekly service to London was also provided.

108 Heybridge Mill, an attractive timber-framed watermill, was demolished about 1950 despite being recognised as being of architectural and historic interest. Once it ground corn into flour for the local farmers. Heybridge Creek, in the foreground, is now permanently dry, having been banked off.

109 A pre-war picture of the Maldon Crystal Salt Company premises, on the site of a medieval salt pan. Although gas now provides the heat for evaporation, when this picture was taken coal furnaces were used, hence the tall chimney.

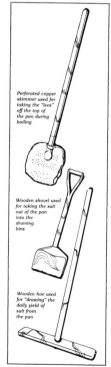

Perforated copper skimmer used for taking the "lees" off the top of the pan during boiling

Wooden shovel used for taking the salt out of the pan into the draining bins

Wooden hoe used for "drawing" the daily yield of salt from the pan

110 An artist's impression of workmen raking out the daily yield of salt from the pan, and sketches of various implements used in salt making.

A traditional scene:- raking or "drawing" the daily yield of salt.

111 One of Bentall's few car advertisements.

112 In all, about one hundred Bentall cars were built. Here, in the automobile assembly shop, they can be seen in various stages of construction.

113 A Bentall test model with a workman at the controls. A packing case is being used as part of the seat and the fascia board is merely a piece of plywood!

114 Described as a 'Standard Side Entrance Car', this 16-20 H.P. Bentall retailed at £327 10s. 0d.

115 (*above*) A copy of an engraving which appeared in a catalogue of 1850, showing the 'Goldhanger' plough, the original product of William Bentall, founder of the firm of E.H. Bentall & Co. Ltd.

116 (*below*) May & Butcher known for ship breaking also manufactured agricultural equipment and implements. Here is their 'Heybridge' pig feeding cowl.

117 (*bottom*) This elaborate thatched pig hut was another May & Butcher product.

GRAY & SONS,

BREWERS & SPIRIT MERCHANTS,

MALDON BREWERY, MALDON.

—:0:—

SPIRITS.

GIN :
Fine Unsweetened.
Booth's.

RUM :
Finest Old Jamaica.

BRANDIES :
Brandy.
Superior French.

WHISKIES :
Irish.
    „   Special Blend.
Scotch, Very Fine Old.

CORDIALS :
Ginger Brandy.
Orange Bitters.
Peppermint.
Cloves.

ALES, PORTER & STOUT.

DESCRIPTION.	Brls. (36 gals.)	Kilds. (18 gals.)	Fir. (9 gals.)	Pins. (4½ gals.)
STOCK ALE :				
XXXO ...	42/-,	21/-,	10/6,	5/3
BITTER ALE :				
B.A. ...	36/-,	18/-,	9/-,	4/6
MILD ALES :				
XXX ...	42/-,	21/-,	10/6,	5/3
XX ...	36/-,	18/-,	9/-,	4/6
STOUT ...	48/-,	24/-,	12/-,	6/-
PORTER ...	36/-,	18/-,	9/-,	4/6

A Discount of 5% allowed for Cash on delivery.

PRICE LIST OF SPIRITS & CORDIALS ON APPLICATION.

L

118 (*above*) Gray & Sons, the Chelmsford-based brewers, were owners of the Maldon Brewery in Gate Street until the 1950s, when it was sold for light industrial purposes. Although Gray's houses still exist locally, they now sell other companies' brews. This advertisement appeared in the last century. The site has now been redeveloped for housing.

119   E.H. Bentall's *Jullamar*, built in 1875 at Heybridge. Its revolutionary design and uncommon yawl rig made her the fastest boat of her class. Her successor *Evolution* was, however, a failure.

120   Workmen gather around a boat under construction in John Howard's boatyard at The Slipways, Maldon.

121 HMS *Dido*, one of the largest vessels to be broken up by May & Butcher at Heybridge Basin. The 5,600-ton light cruiser was launched in 1896 and saw service in the Great War.

122 The bow of HMS *Dido* alongside *Gloria*, an old timber vessel used by May & Butcher in 1926 as a floating base and for housing the breaking gangs. *Gloria* was set ablaze and burned for over two weeks.

123 & 124 (*left and below*) Ship breakers at work.

125 Painting the hull of the sailing yacht *Alpha* at Heybridge Basin, while the barge yacht *Peace* rests on repair blocks.

126 In the 1950s and '60s many sailing barges were dismasted and motorised in a desperate attempt to remain commercially viable. Here, the *Nellie Parker* is seen moored in Cook's boatyard at Maldon; three canoeists ponder their next move.

127 (*above*) A group of workmen engaged in sail dressing at Bradwell earlier this century. Sails were spread out, and a mixture of linseed oil and red ochre was brushed over them, a practice unchanged to this day. The mixture is slow to dry and the workmen's hands and overalls are habitually red-stained. Another man can be seen repairing a sail.

128 (*above right*) A pre-Second World War scene. Drake Brothers, well-known yacht and boat builders at Tollesbury, are seen with a vast array of laid-up yachts and fishing boats. Tollesbury continues as a yachting centre although its fishing industry has declined.

129 (*right*) Maldon's small fleet of inshore fishing craft in the late 1940s waiting for the incoming tide, while sailing dinghies capture the slight breeze. The fishing industry is currently in decline and the few remaining craft are motorised.

Transport — Canal

130 The seal of Chelmer and Blackwater Navigation Company. Its design was inspired by the Naiad Conduit Head, which formerly stood in Tindal Square, Chelmsford. The date on the seal—15 July 1793—commemorates the first meeting of the company at the *Black Boy Hotel*, Chelmsford.

131 A brig locking through Heybridge Basin Sea Lock, *c*.1900, whilst passers-by make fast its painters to the mooring bollards.

132 Sailors and bare-footed children pose on a balance beam at Heybridge Basin Sea Lock, *c*.1880, against a background of towering collier masts. A hoop and stick, a popular children's game of the period, lies discarded at the children's feet.

133 Beeleigh Weir, 1910, where fresh water from the river Blackwater flows into the tidal estuary. This is a pretty place visited by generations of local people for picnics, swimming or fishing.

134 A horse-drawn lighter, *c*.1900, passing Beeleigh Weir on its way to Chelmsford.

135 The canal near Heybridge Basin about 1930, then, as now, a haven for estuary-going yachts and cruisers. Many trees have unfortunately been felled since this photograph was taken.

136 Timber on its way to Chelmsford, *c.*1950. It was laboriously transferred by hand from a dismasted Thames barge to a canal lighter.

137 Heybridge Basin, *c.*1900. In those days it was busy with commercial traffic. A brig has just arrived in the basin whilst a 'stacky' with its load of straw is ready to lock through on its way to London. In the foreground is just a glimpse of two canal lighters waiting for a Chelmsford load.

Railway

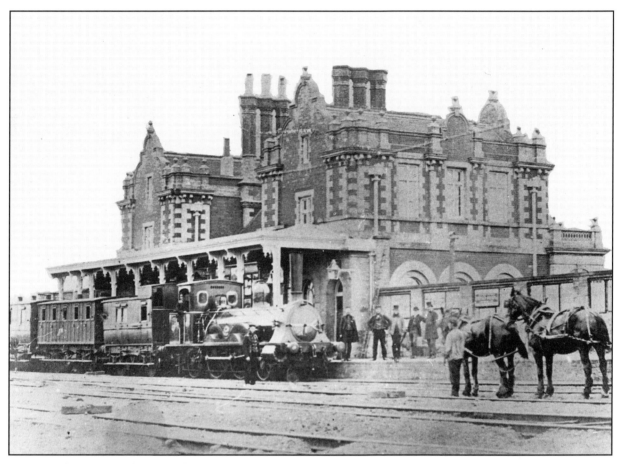

138 Maldon East railway station in the mid-1870s; a passenger train is ready to leave. The locomotive is a 'Scotsman' tank engine, while the carriages are a mixed collection of rolling stock from different ages. The second one is nearly as old as the line itself.

139 Tolleshunt D'Arcy station a few years before 1930. Several passengers and the station master await the approaching train.

140 The same station in 1930. A lorry stands astride the track so that its load can be manhandled onto the platform.

141 8 January 1949, the 12.50 train to Kelvedon about to leave Tollesbury station.

142 View of the interior of a railway carriage which was in operation on the Tollesbury line in 1950. Entry and exit were gained through open verandahs at either end of the carriage.

143 A peaceful scene near Beeleigh *c.*1950, showing the railway viaduct and bridge over the river Chelmer. Although closed, the Maldon West line was being used for the storage of redundant waggons. The central span was removed in 1965. The bridge was completely demolished in the late 1980s when Maldon bypass was built on the same alignment as the former railway. The replacement bridge has been designed to echo the appearance of the old bridge by the use of similar facing materials.

Road

144 Delivering timber in pre-war days.

145 The Eastern National's bus station, soon after its construction in the 1930s. It was built in a style similar to that of other stations erected at Chelmsford, Clacton and Halstead at about the same time.

146 The interior of the Eastern National bus garage at the rear of the station, prior to the Second World War, with several different types of single-decker bus and a double-decker. The latter could only be used on a few routes because of the limited headroom of many road bridges.

Events

147 This picture of Beeleigh Falls was taken in 1905, when a spell of cold weather almost halted the flow of water through the sluices into the tidal estuary.

148 The estuary at Maldon frozen over during what must have been an exceptionally hard winter. A gentleman surveys the arctic scene, whilst his dog waits patiently to continue the walk.

149 Both the river Chelmer and the river Blackwater, after heavy rain each winter, are prone to burst their banks, and water spreads over the adjacent meadows. Here, in a very rare summer flood, the water can be seen cascading over Beeleigh Weir.

150 In January 1928, Heybridge Basin suffered a serious flood despite the protection offered by the sea wall. In some places there was up to a foot of flood water and some people were forced to go shopping by rowing boat.

151 Territorial soldiers, prior to the Great War, marching from Maldon West station on their way to Wycke for training.

152 A military band approaches the Moot Hall during the Great War, followed by columns of soldiers, while townspeople line the pavements.

153 The Bishop of Barking dedicates the Great War Memorial outside All Saints' Church, watched by members of the British Legion and other local people.

154 The community at Heybridge Basin was once almost isolated, and when a villager died the funeral cortège was a very stately affair, travelling by canal lighter upstream to Heybridge cemetery.

155 A show of agricultural machinery at The Causeway, *c.*1910, which attracted large numbers of local farmers. Both the Maldon Iron Works and Bentall's were represented, as were Joslin of Colchester and J. Brittain Pash of Chelmsford.

People

156 George Sains, his horse Charlie, and a milk float from the Half Way Dairy ready to take part in the Maldon Carnival, *c*.1920.

157 Edward Hammond Bentall, born 1814 and died 1898. Under this great innovator the Bentall factory expanded its products, which were sold all over Great Britain and the Empire. He was a Liberal M.P. for Maldon from 1868 to 1876, commanded a Volunteer Unit at Heybridge and was the founder Commodore of the Blackwater Sailing Club.

158 At the Essex agricultural shows held during the 1920s and '30s May & Butcher exhibited their farm and garden equipment. Here, Miss Nora Butcher, a daughter of one of the firm's partners, relaxes after a successful day.

159 Sitting together in front of an ex-army bell tent at the Essex agricultural show are George Butcher and a May & Butcher employee. The tent was probably erected to provide wet weather accommodation.

160 The Maldon Grammar School hockey team in the 1920s. Back row: A. Bromhead, B. Stevens, N. Butcher, M. Calderbank. Front row: J. Barford, E. Goodwin, E. Dowling.

150.

161 (*top left*) A group of canal employees pause in their maintenance work at Beeleigh Lock, *c*.1938. The canal foreman, William Siggers, stands in the centre of the lighter.

162 (*above*) Men of Maldon's part-time voluntary fire brigade in 1923 proudly display their first motorised fire engine.

163 (*left*) During the Great War large numbers of troops were stationed in East Anglia in case of invasion. They were kept at a high state of alert with constant training to keep fit. Here, men of the 4th Battalion of the Essex Regiment receive final instructions before the start of their cross-country run from their camp at Maldon, *c*.1915.

164 This carefully posed studio portrait of a young man was taken in Mr. Gladwin's studio in Maldon, clearly as a family memento.

165 A young woman in a broderie anglaise blouse and skirt. Her exceptionally large wrist watch is, in fact, a gentleman's fob watch set into a leather strap. The time is four o'clock. Dark stockings and button over shoes complete the picture, taken in about 1910 at the Electric Studio, Market Hill.

166 A Victorian lady photographed by F. Edwards of Market Hill, wearing a black bombazine fringed jacket and skirt with plumed matching hat. Jet brooch and earrings complete the picture, possibly recently widowed.

167 James Spitty, wearing a sou'wester, was one-time landlord of the beerhouse *The Case is Altered* of Bradwell waterside. A man of many parts, he was also a bargeman.

References

Benham, Hervey, *Down Tops'l*
Benham, Hervey, *Last Stronghold of Sail*
Chelmsford Advertiser
Essex Countryside
Essex Record Office, *Maldon—A Pictorial History*
Fitch, E.A., *Maldon and the Blackwater Estuary*
Great Eastern Journal, No.11 July 1977
History of John Sadd Ltd., booklet
Kemp, P.K., *The Bentall Story*
Maldon and Burnham Standard, various issues
Maldon Crystal Salt Co. Ltd., leaflet
Maldon District Council, *The Maldon District*
Maldon Maritime Trail, leaflet
Marriage, John, *Barging into Chelmsford*, 1993
Marriage, John, 'Maldon—a redevelopment scheme', unpublished thesis
Swindale, Dennis, *Branch Lines to Maldon*
Tait, H. Joy, *The Ancient Borough of Maldon*
White, Archie, *Tideways and Byways in Essex and Suffolk*
White, W., *History, Gazetteer and Directory of the County of Essex*, 1848

Index

Roman numerals refer to pages in the Introduction, and arabic numerals to individual illustrations.

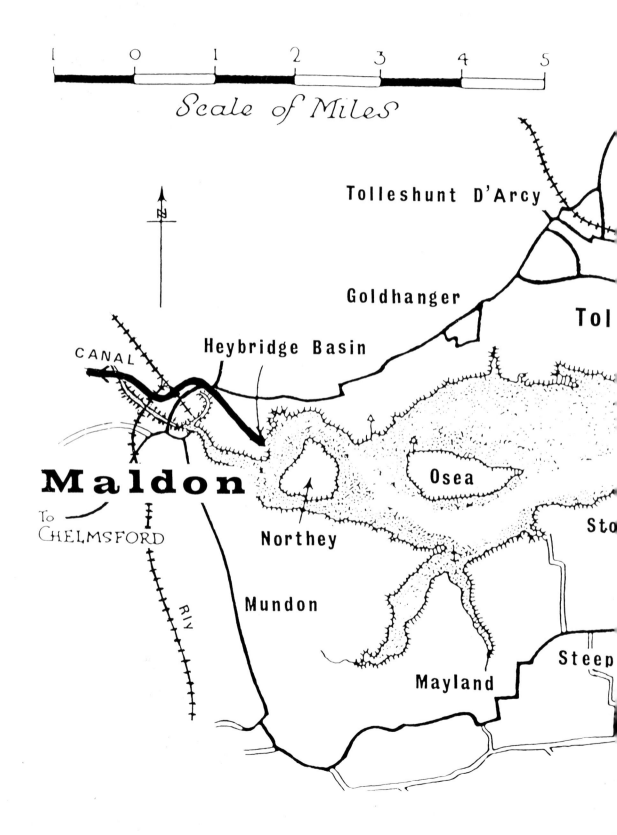

BLACKWATER

Scale of Miles

1 0 1 2 3 4 5

Tolleshunt D'Arcy

Goldhanger

Tol

Heybridge Basin

CANAL

Maldon

To
CHELMSFORD

RIV

Northey

Osea

Sto

Mundon

Mayland

Steep